Sever
Organic Vegetable Garden

The Basic Steps to Make Anyone a Green Thumb Gardener

Mike Cunningham
The Teaching Farmer of Country Gardens Farm

ISBN # 978-1535123785

Acknowledgments

I would like to thank my wife Judy for all her help and encouragement in life and in writing this book. Judy and I have been married for 38 years and a 7 year courtship before that, starting in high school. Through all those years she has worked beside me and supported me in all that we have done in our nursery business and on our farm.

I would also like to thank those that came before me. My family and friends and neighbors have paved the way for us to make a living farming and to write this book.

My mom Cornelia is a great gardener and helped me to start my first plant nursery when I was a teenager. She continues to be there to help in the greenhouse, seeding and planting many thousands of plants. Thanks Mom.

My dad Thad passed away several years ago. He loved to farm and that lives on in me to this day. I can't help but think that if he was living he would enjoy seeing our farm and his grandsons continuing to do what he loved.

My Grandparents both on my mom's side and dad's were farmers. I have a lot of good memories of them growing vegetable gardens and flowers around their homes. My grandmother Couch was always digging up plants to pass along to us to be planted at our home. My grandmother Cunningham (Sagie) would show me how to start plants from seeds and cuttings on her front porch. My grandfather Couch had a very neat vegetable garden just out the back door of their house. I was amazed as a kid as I watched him dig peanuts from his garden. My grandfather Cunningham (Pop) was not able to garden because of his health when I came along but I am grateful to him for the farm he bought back in 1940 that we farm today.

Judy's mom and dad also were farmers and I learned a lot from them about working together as a team on the farm and raising a family. Judy's dad would have me working in their chicken house with the rest of the family when I would come over to see Judy. They were always about hard work but it did not seem hard because of the way they always had fun and helped each other finish their chores every day.

I was fortunate enough to have two neighbors that were great gardeners.

Smokey Sullivan was a very inventive farmer. If he did not have a tool he would make one. I remember he would sometimes come by our farm and when he saw us struggling with some job we were doing, he would go back to his shop and make a better tool for us to use.

Ralph Segrest was a Methodist preacher who loved to garden. When I was a kid he would show me how to divide the perennials he grew in his flower garden. His vegetable garden was always beautiful and even though I know he worked very hard in it, he always made it look easy.

I consider myself to have a good life and have had several close friends that have enriched my life.

John Alexander and I have baled hay, chased cows, birthed calves and worked together for many years. When our boys grew up and stopped showing cows in 4-H, we did not want to stop so we started raising grass fed beef together. Thanks John for all your help and support over the years and for being a close friend.

I have some friends that don't farm or garden but never-the-less have been a great influence to me. Tim and Jodi Smith encouraged me to write this book and held me accountable by asking each week, "How much did you get done on the book this week?"

Tim and I have been friends for a long time. He was the city boy that I always brought into my activities on the farm like pig raising and Fourth of July home grown whole hog bar-b-ques. Thanks Tim and Jodi for your encouragement and friendship.

Two other people that I must mention that helped me get this book completed are Deberah Williams, and Karla Cunningham that helped with the editing and formatting of this book.

Thanks to Glenn Eric Naylor for the Illustrations.

Seven Steps to an Organic Vegetable Garden

Introduction

Just like many things that are rewarding and fulfilling, vegetable gardening can be frustrating as well. People will say about a successful gardener "they must have a green thumb because they can grow anything," Truth is — just like with any sport, hobby, or occupation — it takes time and practice to hone your skill. Gardening is no different than any other endeavor. That is, you must get the basic fundamentals down in order to be successful.

In this book I want to give you the fundamentals of vegetable gardening. Even if you have been gardening for years and now you want to garden organically keeping a basic understanding about how plants grow will help you to be more successful.

I have had a love for growing plants ever since my Grandmother first planted the seed of gardening in me on her front porch when I was just a kid. In my 50 years of gardening, I have killed many plants and have had many crop failures that have taught me how to be successful more times than not.

I love to see things grow. It is just the way I am wired. I see that same love in others as well even if they are not gardeners. When you see a beautiful garden it is satisfying. It may be a manicured garden that man has made or a natural setting of God's hand. A garden is food for the soul whether you consume it with your eyes or your mouth. After all, God first placed us in the Garden of Eden and I think that we have a deep desire within us to return to the garden.

So begin your journey into gardening knowing that plants have been growing on this earth since time began and usually have done quite well without our help. Producing the kinds of vegetables that we desire to eat for our benefit is what we are coaxing our garden to provide. Notice that I said coaxing, not forcing. We want to work with nature not against it.

Growing our own food has many benefits. We get to enjoy the process of seeing plants grow then we get to enjoy it a second time as we eat that food for the nourishment of our bodies. Sharing a meal with friends and family that has come from something you have grown is fulfilling. Food just tastes better, tastes fresher and is more nutritious when we grow it ourselves.

Kids are much more likely to eat something they have helped grow or pick from the garden. When we have kids come out to the farm and we have carrots growing I always let them pull up a carrot. This is just amazing to them, that a carrot is pulled from the ground. Sometimes they are a little bit troubled because it has dirt on it but once we take them over to the water faucet and wash it off 9 out of 10 kids will eat their carrot right there in the garden. We have still got to work on that 1 out of 10 picky eaters!

When I say you should grow your own food I don't mean that you have to grow all of your food. Grow as much or as little as you have the time and resources for. A few pots of herbs on the back deck may be your speed and that's OK. It is better to start small than to dive in the deep water before you are ready to swim.

What I want to show you in this book is how to get started and how to learn the basics of growing an *Organic* vegetable garden. First of all, an organic garden is not a garden of neglect. If you just throw out a few seeds and hope for the best you will have limited success. Organic gardening is a holistic approach to growing plants. If you provide all the necessary things a plant needs to be healthy it will not be as susceptible to insects and diseases.

We can't control everything — especially the weather. The basic needs for plants are light, air, nutrients, correct temperature and moisture. To the extent that we can provide these things in the correct amounts that each particular variety needs then we will have healthier plants, less insects and diseases and more production of vegetables.

In an organic garden, plants depend on the good bugs to keep down the harmful bug population and for pollination so we don't want to kill all the insects. Our remedies even if organic need to be used with care so that we don't harm the beneficial insects in our garden.

The beneficial microorganisms in the soil are another consideration and should be seen as an asset to the plants and managed properly.

As you think about growing an organic garden don't just think of the garden that is absent of synthetic chemicals, but think of how you can make the garden the healthiest it can be by natural means. In this book, I will cover the seven steps necessary to help you grow your own organic vegetable garden.

Step 1: Location

Psalm 1:3 (NIV)
That person is like a tree planted by streams of water,
which yields its fruit in season
and whose leaf does not wither—
whatever they do prospers.

7.29.17. GEN.

Bloom where you are planted is a phrase I see quoted sometimes. I think I resemble that quote. Pop (what we called my Dad's father) moved his family to the land Judy and I farm now in the early 40's. He was what they called then a truck farmer. He grew vegetables and loaded them on his truck and took them to the State Farmers Market in Atlanta.

After my dad came home from WWII he married my mother and they lived in Decatur, near Atlanta. A few years later I came along and my Dad wanted to come back to the farm in Newnan so the only place I have ever lived that I can remember is where I live now. After Judy and I married we built a couple of houses and raised our 4 sons but we have never lived over a mile away from where we live now.

By the time I came along I can only remember Pop being sick a lot and not being able to farm very much. My grandmother who we called Sagie on the other hand was an active gardener growing flowers and vegetables mainly for our family. I remember she and my mother working in the family garden, picking, cooking and canning every summer.

I must have liked my location because 60 years later I am still here. In my part of Georgia the weather is not always perfect. It is hot and humid in the summer and can have sudden cold spells in the winter. The soil is mostly red clay and not always easy to garden in but overall it has been a great place to live and raise a family. I even have found ways to overcome the heat and the cold and the red clay to grow some really productive gardens.

So wherever you find yourself and whatever obstacles you may face in life just find a way to:

Bloom where you are planted.

Full sun

The best location will have full sun or at least 6 to 8 hours of full sun a day. Less than that and you can grow leafy greens like lettuce, but don't expect much from plants that produce a root or a fruit crop like carrots or tomatoes.

Avoid tree roots

In choosing your location, avoid tree roots because not only will there likely be a tree nearby to shade your garden but the roots can grow into your vegetable beds and pots and drain the moisture and nutrients. Not to mention they can make it impossible to work the soil. Even if you build your beds above tree roots they can invade your gardening space over time.

Evaluate your soil quality

Good garden soil is sometimes hard to come by so if you have it naturally, then count yourself lucky. Don't worry, if you have soil that is rock hard clay or if your soil is more like beach sand - you can fix it. Refer to Step 3 on soils for what to do.

Evaluate the surface drainage

Are you at the bottom of the hill where water stands? Not good.

Is your area you want to use flat but water stands because it has nowhere to go? That can be a problem, too. You want an area that slopes slightly where water does not collect. If your area needs drainage, you may need to put in French drains, ditches or do some light grading. Raised beds will also help to get you above a wet area but try to get the surface water to drain away.

Evaluate the soil percolation

This is how fast the water drains into the soil instead of the surface drainage that runs off your site. You can do a test by digging a 12 inch deep hole where you want your garden and fill it with water. Check it in 12 hours and measure how much has drained out. You want a minimum of 1/2 an inch an hour to drain so in 12 hours you should have 6 inches or less of the original 12 inches that you put in. This is less important if you are going to be growing in raised beds or pots where you would be filling with soil that you bring in.

Look for problem weeds

When deciding on the location of your garden, look for problematic weeds. Perennial weeds are much harder to eradicate than annual weeds. So weeds like Bermuda grass, nut grass, and woody vines will have to be completely removed or you will be fighting them every year. Annual weeds are weeds that come up from seed every year like crabgrass, chickweed and pig-weed and can be removed much easier. Stay away from the hard to control perennial weeds if you have a choice when picking out a garden spot.

Locate your garden near a water source

Even if you live in an area that gets lots of rainfall you will need to water your garden from time to time. Having a water source that is nearby and easy to access is a great benefit. Installing drip irrigation in the beginning is a great idea. Drip irrigation is water that is delivered directly to the roots of the plant by a small plastic pipe that lies on top of the ground or slightly under it and drips out slowly so that the water soaks in instead of evaporating or running off giving the maximum benefit to the plant. It also keeps the leaves of the plant dry when you are watering discouraging fungal diseases that are made worse by wet leaves.

Visibility

Locate your garden where it is easy for you to see it every day. You will be making frequent trips to harvest and maintain your garden so closer is better.

The location you choose may not be perfect but you can adjust many things. Poor soil, bad drainage, troublesome weeds, and access to water can be overcome. The hardest thing to overcome is not enough sun. If you don't have enough sun you may be limited to growing leafy greens or you may want to consider having a plot at a community garden if you have one nearby.

Takeaway Points

Here are the key points that I want you to remember about locating your garden.

▶ **Locating in the full sun is best, at least 6 to 8 hours of direct sun a day**

▶ **Evaluate the soil quality**

▶ **Avoid areas where water does not drain away**

▶ **Evaluate the percolation (your soil needs to absorb at least a 1/2 inch of water per hour**

▶ **Locate close to a water source so it is convenient to water your garden**

▶ **Locate away from hard to control weeds**

▶ **Locate away from trees**

▶ **Locate in an area where it is convenient to check on it regularly**

▶ **A garden is a lot like a pet. It doesn't require a lot of time every day but it can't be neglected for days at a time. You would not leave your dog unattended while you go on vacation so don't leave your garden unattended either.**

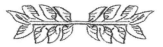

Step 2: Making Beds or Using Containers

Luke 14:28 (NIV)
"Suppose one of you wants to build a tower. Will he not first set down and estimate the cost to see if he has enough money to complete it? "

The first time I saw someone make a raised garden bed by building a wooden box on the ground I thought how silly that is. Over the years I have built many of those silly boxes and even planted small vegetable gardens in pots. I suppose the lesson in that is don't knock it until you try it.

I was in Brazil on a mission trip several years ago and was visiting some local small farms and this one farmer was growing cilantro in raised beds. All his raised beds were made by lining the sides with liquor and wine bottles. He stood them upright to border the garden bed and hold his good soil in place. All the glass bottles with their different colors of glass made for an attractive site. He was doing what my grandmother Sagie would say is making do with what you have.

My wife Judy likes to grow herbs on our farm and I am always stopping her from putting them in the vegetable fields because some herbs like mint can be very aggressive and take over where you don't want them. I just really don't like a little diddle of this and that getting in my way when I am ready to plant.

We have reached a compromise and we grow lots of herbs that she plants in pots and even baby swimming pools filled with soil.

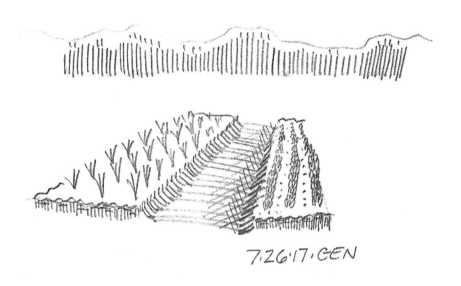

7.26.17.GEN

Whether you want to grow on flat ground or soil mounding up with no border around it at all or the most expensive material you can buy to border your raised beds just count the cost and make do with what you have.

Unless you are cultivating a large garden with some type of

mechanical equipment, it is much more efficient to plant in wide beds rather than individual rows. Whether you build your beds with some type of material to make raised beds or you make wide beds in the ground from the native soil you have, you want to make your beds no wider than you can reach from either side – 3 to 4 foot wide beds are usually the standard. There is also no reason why you cannot grow some or all your garden in pots.

Making Raised Beds

First, let's look at making raised beds with different materials. I have used wooden boards 8 inches wide and 4 foot, 8 foot, 10 foot or 12 foot long. I don't use treated wood because I want to be totally organic. I have seen 2 inch thick untreated pine last for 4 years or more. Wood from Cedar, Cypress, and Oak are more rot-resistant than Pine or Spruce, but are also more expensive.

Other materials for making raised beds include Rock, Brick, Block, and man-made Stone that is used in making retaining walls. I have also seen composite boards like the ones used to make outdoor decks as well as some that were made out of sheets of metal roofing standing on its side in a frame to make a deep bed. There are as many possibilities as there are building materials.

I have also seen raised beds so tall you don't have to bend over to plant in them and others only 4 or 6 inches deep. I like to plant into beds at least 8 inches deep. Remember, the deeper the bed, the more soil it takes to fill it. Taller beds on legs work great for the elderly and the handicapped and you can find plans for those types of beds on-line.

Row Cover

Having a frame to attach metal or PVC pipe to makes it easy to cover your garden beds with row cover to protect it from frost or insect damage.

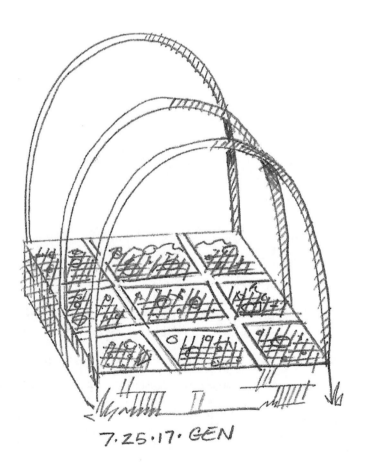

7.25.17. GEN

Row cover is a spun material that comes in different weights. The heavier row cover is used to protect from the cold and the lighter row covers protect crops from insects while allowing up to 80% of the sunlight through. This is a great tool for organically controlling insects as long as they don't need pollination. On crops that don't need pollination like leafy greens and broccoli you can leave the cover on all season. On crops like squash you would need to take it off when you see the first blooms.

These bows can also support netting or wire to keep out critters like deer and rabbits. To make these bows over a 4 foot wide bed, use 10 foot long, 1/2 inch PVC pipe and attach with a 3/4 inch, two-hole pipe strap along your side board. If you want to use metal conduit you would need a jig to bend the 1/2 inch metal but the PVC can be bent easily by hand. The benefit of using the metal conduit is that it will last much longer than the PVC, but the PVC will last for several years before becoming brittle in the sun and breaking.

Containers

Containers can be a good alternative for growing herbs and vegetables. Almost any container that has drainage holes can be used to grow in. Larger vegetables like tomatoes and peppers need a container that holds 4 or 5 gallons of soil, but smaller plants like lettuce and herbs can be grown in much smaller pots.

You can use other potting soil that has good drainage but you

7.27.17 . GEN .

may need to add an organic fertilizer. I use Mike's Mix potting soil for my containers and raised beds (See Step 3 on soils).

If you are growing in both raised beds and containers you can plant things that don't take up much room like lettuce, spinach, and carrots in your raised beds. Vegetables that grow large or have trailing vines like tomatoes, squash and melons can be planted in individual containers. That way, you can either trellis the large plants or let them run along the ground and not take over the space in your raised bed. One watermelon plant can take over a 4x4 raised bed.

Containers take more attention because they will dry out faster than plants in the ground. I have used drip irrigation on timers to water my containers so that they are not drying out all the time. Applying the water a slow rate right on the roots of the plant is a good idea for watering all your plants and you can read more about that in Step 5.

Containers are also a good way to start small if you are a beginner or you have limited space. The other advantage to using containers is that they are mobile and as the angle of the sun changes you can move your containers around to get the maximum exposure they need.

Straw Bale Gardening

Straw bale gardening is another gardening method that has become popular with some people lately. This is where you line up straw bales on their sides and add fertilizer and a little potting soil to the bale to initiate the rotting process of the straw bale. As the straw begins to break down you plant into the potting soil that you put on the bale. The plant roots eventually grow into the straw bale, taking up nutrients as the straw rots. The advantages of using this method are that you have little or no weeds, low cost for startup and an instant raised bed. The disadvantages are that it may not be easy to find a chemical free straw bale and the straw dries out really fast.

Takeaway Points

Here are the key points I want you to remember about beds and containers.

▶ **You don't have to border your beds with anything to make a raised bed. They can simply be mounded up in the middle with slightly sloping sides.**

▶ **You can use many different kinds of materials to border your beds but try to stay away from pressure treated wood.**

▶ **Bordering your beds has advantages like weed control. Also borders keep all your soil in place. Building a box makes it possible to have taller beds with less bending and it gives a clean tidy look.**

▶ **Containers are useful for several reasons. They are good for growing sprawling plants that would otherwise take over an entire raised bed. They can be moved around to take advantage of the best sun exposure. They are a good way for beginners or those that have limited space to start gardening.**

▶ **Beds that are planted 3 to 4 foot wide are more space efficient than single rows of plants with walkways in-between.**

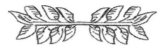

Step 3: Soil

Ezekiel 17:8 (NIV)
It had been planted in good soil by abundant water so that it would produce branches, bear fruit and become a splendid vine.'

Our topsoil may be the most valuable natural resource that we have in this world. There are more living organisms in a handful of good garden soil than there are people that are alive in the world today.

There is life in this thin crust of soil covering our planet and it is what provides our food. It is nourishment for all the plants that grow on earth. Even the oxygen that plants produce is dependent on this living layer of soil that some people just call dirt.

I remember as a young boy loving to have my bare feet in the soil. I would sometimes walk behind the tractor as my dad would be plowing and step just behind the plow and let the warm soil cover my bare feet.

I recently read that some people believe that we should be having more contact with the earth with our bare hands and feet. They call it grounding. So I guess I knew what I was doing when I would walk through a freshly plowed field bare foot but I just didn't know you called it grounding.

The soil has a smell and a taste. Yes I said taste and before you say you should not be putting soil in your mouth I will tell you that I raised 4 strapping sons and I saw them with soil in their mouths more times than I can remember. That is what an immune system is for.

I love the smell of warm garden soil in the spring. It has a unique smell and once you know that smell you can recognize it every time. Some may say that I spend way too much time thinking about soil but it is what gives life to the plants we grow. Although we can't control some things in gardening like the weather we can always do things to improve the soil.

So we should treasure our soil and do everything we can to improve it and not just treat it like dirt.

Location

After picking a sunny location, the next most important step is to consider the soil you are going to grow in. The soil is the stomach of the plant and it is the key to a healthy organic garden. Spend your time and money on this step and it will reward you with a bountiful garden. If you don't pay attention to your soil you will be plagued with problems.

Every gardener instinctively knows that you need good soil if you want your garden to flourish. There is always advice handed out that if you buy some bag of this or potions of that it will solve all your problems and give you good soil. What I have experienced is that it is not any one thing that is the answer. It is a holistic approach of providing good things for your soil.

Let's look at what good soil is.

▶ Feels soft and crumbles easily
▶ Drains well
▶ Warms up quickly in the spring
▶ Does not crust over
▶ Has few clods and no hardpan
▶ Soaks up heavy rains with little runoff
▶ Stores moisture during periods of drought
▶ Resists erosion and nutrient loss
▶ Supports a high population of soil organisms
▶ Has a rich earthy smell
▶ Does not require increasing inputs for high yields
▶ Produces healthy, high quality crops

Raise your hand if you have this kind of soil. Likely not; unless you are blessed to live in a minority of places on earth or you have been taking good care of your soil for years.

Good soil is a thing to be treasured and managed. It is like a relationship that has to be nurtured because if neglected and abused, it will stop giving and yielding the luscious crops you desire.

When I talk about soil in the garden, I break it into two categories. One is the native mineral soil that you have on your property. It was there before you and is made from the minerals and rocks that have been breaking down for ages. If you are lucky, it also has some organic material from living things that are now decomposed. Having 5% organic material in the soil is considered good, but very hard to get and maintain. The second category of garden soil is what I call potting soil. You usually buy this in a bag and it can contain things like peat moss, perlite, vermiculite, composted manure and ground or composted bark to name a few. I will discuss potting soil later but for now I will focus on Mineral soil.

In my part of the country, the Piedmont of Georgia, we are either blessed or cursed with clay soil; however you choose to look at it. Clay contains many minerals and will hold on to nutrients for the plants to use but it is also can be hard to work with. Never try to dig it when it is wet because that will leave it as hard as a brick and take years to recover. It is as sticky as peanut butter when wet and cracks open when too dry. It can be so compacted that it lacks enough oxygen to support good plant growth and is usually very low in organic matter. This is the soil that I have gardened in all my life and the best thing that you can do to improve it is to add organic matter to it. If it is a small area, you buy enough compost to cover the ground 2 to 3 inches deep and till it in. The other way is to grow your compost in the form of cover crops like clover, iron clay peas, vetch, rye or oats. These crops can be chopped up and tilled in to decompose thereby adding their rich matter back to the soil. Animal manures and other organic byproducts like wood chips and leaves are also good sources of organic matter. Basically anything that was once alive and now is dead and decaying is good for the soil.

Improving the Soil

The good thing is that improving the soil by adding organic matter works well with clay soils and sandy soils. There may be other adjustments you need to make so I encourage everyone to take a soil sample which we will discuss later.

The soil is the stomach of the plant and all minerals and nutrients have to be digested in the soil so that the plant can take them up. Having good soil that is teaming with good microorganisms and the other attributes listed above is a joy to work with and will head off many other problems that gardens encounter. Pay attention to the soil and your plants will thrive.

If you are buying mineral soil (native top soil) it can be hard to come by so go take a look at it before ordering a truck load over the phone. It should look like something you have seen in a local garden before. If you are buying bulk, you may be able to get the landscape supply yard to mix compost with your top soil for you. I like a ratio of 1/3 compost to 2/3 top soil. Always ask the source of your top soil and compost. Stay away from treated sewage waste. It is okay for lawns and flowers, but should not be used in a food garden.

I have never seen mineral top soil in bags mainly because it is too heavy to ship. Most things marked topsoil are composted bark which in itself is not bad but it is not native mineral topsoil.

The least expensive and most efficient way to start your garden is to use the soil you have now. Any soil will benefit by adding compost. You want to add about 3 inches of compost across the top of your garden bed and mix or till it in. You can also take a couple of inches of your topsoil that would be in the walkways and add it to your beds. This works if you are making permanent raised beds and the walkways will stay in the same place. See making the beds in step 2.

Potting Soil

Growing in containers and raised beds are good options for many gardeners. Some of the benefits include less space required, less weeding, quick setup and movable pots that can be placed on hard surfaces or hard ground. Besides the box or pot that you will use to grow your vegetables in you will need some type of soil. In my 40 plus years of growing plants in containers there is one thing that holds true – once you put soil into a container it behaves very differently than the soil that is in the ground. Mainly the drainage has to be much better in a container or the soil will hold too much water and the plants will suffer. The swings between wet and dry soil are more dramatic. Potting soil will either dry out too fast or stay wet too long depending on how well it drains and what it is made of.

Some time back in the 50's and 60's nurserymen starting putting more plants in containers and they needed a soil mix that was light and drained well. The mix that was used was called a soilless mix because it contained no mineral or native soil. Instead, soilless media was made from organic materials like peat moss, composted pine bark, perlite, and vermiculite or other non-soil amendments. Today we can buy these potting soil mixes in a variety of recipes and brand names. I have always liked the peat moss based potting soils but I am beginning to try some mixes that substitute peat with coir. Coir is a ground coconut husk which is a renewable resource and is said to support microorganisms better than peat moss. Until I am more familiar with how to use the coir all my recommendations will be using peat moss.

My Recipe

The recipe I use now for growing vegetables works well in a pot or a raised bed like a square foot garden. Be sure your pot has drainage holes. The recipe I show below is one that I have used many times with good results. The amounts in this recipe are enough to fill a 4×4 square foot garden, 7 inches deep. If you use 8 inch wide dimensional lumber to make your beds the finished size is actually 7-1/2 inches. The brand names I use are what is available in my area and I am sure could be substituted as long as they are similar. Every cook will tweak a recipe to make it his own and I am no different with my soil recipe so this is not the only potting soil that will work but it is the one that has worked well for me.

What is in Mike's Mix?

▶ **Sunshine #1 natural & organic potting soil.** This potting soil contains 70% Canadian sphagnum, peat moss, coarse Perlite, dolomitic limestone, organic wetting agent. It is an OMRI listed soil and can be used in organic production. It comes in a loose fill 2.8 cubic foot bag. This is a product sold by Sungro Horticultural in their professional line so you would need to get it from an independent garden center or greenhouse that could order it for you. We try to keep it on hand and sell it from our farm in Newnan, Georgia. You can read about it online at Sungro.

▶ **Black Kow** is a brand and they sell cow manure compost and Black Kow mushroom compost. Black Kow is composted cow manure and Black Kow Mushroom Compost is composted chicken manure that was used to grow mushrooms then bagged and sold as mushroom compost. By using two different types of compost in your potting soil you will get a wider range of nutrients and minerals. You can read about it online at Black Kow.

▶ **Organic Fertilizer.** We use organic composted chicken manure fertilizer 3-2-3 for most plants and feather meal 7-1-1 for the plants that use higher nitrogen.

▶ **AZOMITE** is a rock powder that contains a wide assortment of minerals. The name stands for A to Z of Minerals in the Earth. We use these minerals every time we plant on the farm and in our potting soil. We also sell this at our farm in Newnan, Georgia or go online to find a dealer near you. Azomite

▶ **Worm Castings.** We started using worm castings in our potting soil years ago and notice a big difference in plant growth and disease resistance. Worm castings are basically worm poop which contains beneficial microorganisms for your plants. We don't use as much as we do compost because of the price but think of it as a probiotic to inoculate the soil. Look for a local source, maybe someone that is growing worms for bait. Some bags of worm castings have fillers of peat moss and are cheaper, but you get what you pay for. We have worm castings available here at Country Gardens Farm that we produce on the farm.

Mike's Mix Recipe

Here are the amounts that you will need to mix up approximately 10 cubic ft. (enough to fill a 4 ft. X 4 ft. bed that is 7 inches deep).

2 bags of Sunshine Organic Potting Soil (each bag is 2.8 cu ft)
2 bags of Black Kow Cow Manure Compost (40 pound bags approximately 1 cu ft per bag)
2 bags of Black Kow Mushroom Compost (40 pound bags approximately 1 cu ft per bag)
3 pounds of Organic Fertilizer 3-2-3
1 pound Azomite
4 quarts worm castings

The easiest way I have found to mix these ingredients together is to spread out a 10 ft. X 10 ft. tarp next to where you are going to use the soil. Thoroughly mix together all ingredients with a shovel and add just enough water to make the mix damp but not too wet. Shovel this into your garden bed. It can also be stored in a trash can for later use.

Soil Test

Why test your soil? In my experience I have found that if I know more about the soil in my garden the more I can adjust the nutrients so my plants will grow to their full potential. We can tell a lot of things about the soil by observing it. But to have hard numbers about PH, minerals and organic matter content I have always sent soil samples off to a soil lab. In every state I know of they have state run soil labs that will test your soil very inexpensively. Or for not much more, you can use a private lab and usually get more detailed information. If you are gardening in virgin native soil you will most likely need to adjust the PH of the soil. If you are buying potting soil in a bag it has usually been PH adjusted already.

Other useful information a soil test will give you is the current availability of minerals in the soil, phosphorus and potassium being the two main ones. The soil test will not tell you about minerals that are in the soil that are not yet available to plants so don't be discouraged if your minerals are low because over time good microorganisms in the soil will break down more minerals and make them available to the plant. This is where knowing the percentage of organic matter in the soil is important because healthy soil with a balanced PH of around 6.5 and at least 3% to 5% organic matter content will increase the microorganisms in the soil. This in turn will break down more minerals that are in the soil and make them useful to the plant.

What is PH?

What is PH and why should I care about it? Our body has an ideal PH and in fact, we cannot vary from the ideal very much or we would die. The soil has a PH and plants perform best when it is in a certain range. PH is a way of expressing the acidity or the alkalinity of something. It has a value between 1 and 14 with 1 being the most acidic and 14 being the most alkaline and 7 being neutral. With the exception of a few acid loving plants like blueberries and azaleas, most plants do their best in a PH of 6.5 just on the acidic side of neutral.

In Georgia where I live, our soils are naturally acidic around 5 to 5.5 and we want to raise that to 6.5 for our vegetable gardens to be the most successful. Basically, nutrients are more available to the plant at the right PH. A lot of times adding good compost to the soil will help balance the PH but mostly we need to add limestone. Other base materials like potassium raise PH as well but I find it less expensive to use a finely ground limestone. Limestone is a natural rock found in many parts of the country and is considered organic.

To determine if and how much limestone you need you first need to do a soil test. You do this by taking several core samples of soil 4 to 6 inches deep all over your garden and mixing these cores of soil together to get a random sample. If there is one area in your garden that you know has been treated differently in the amount of compost or other amendments that you have already added then you may want to do those areas separately. You can send your soil sample off to a lab to get it tested. Most counties have a university extension service that can send off your sample to get it tested. There are also some private labs that will test your soil as well. Once you get the results back it will usually come with a recommendation on how much lime or other amendments you need to balance your soil correctly.

It takes a lot of lime to move the PH one point. It takes approximately 50 pounds of limestone per 1000 square feet to change from a 5.5 to 6.5 on the PH scale. It also takes time to correct PH. Applying lime several months ahead of the crops you want to grow is the best practice. Tilling lime into the soil will distribute it better than lying on top of the soil but spreading it on the top of the soil will also work.

In some parts of the country it is possible for the PH to be too high (above 7) and in that case you could use soil Sulfur to bring the PH down. Consult your state agricultural university for local recommendations.

Adding Fertilizer to the Soil

Fertilizer sold in bags has three numbers on it whether it is organic or chemical (synthetic). The first number is Nitrogen the second number is phosphorus and the third number is potassium. These three nutrients are used by the plant more than any others. The other minerals are also important but in much less quantity. You can think about it this way. You could not live on just taking vitamins. You would still need proteins and carbohydrates to stay alive and the N, P, K, in fertilizer is what the plant needs in larger quantities just like you need carbs and proteins. You soil test will tell you exactly what you need of each. If you don't have a soil test then the recommendations on the fertilizer bag will work. We use rock powders like Azomite and Limestone to supply our minor and trace minerals to the plant. You will also get these minerals from your compost but it has been my experience that not all but most compost comes up short in supplying everything you need for good plant growth. One good way to apply fertilizer is to start off with a half the recommended application and add the rest as the plant grows every two weeks.

So what is organic fertilizer? If it was once alive or it is a mineral from the earth then it can be organic. Organic fertilizer is not mixed or treated with a chemical like chlorine or acid. Cow manure was once grass or grain that the cow ate so it was once alive as a plant. Phosphorus is a mineral in the earth and is organic until it is treated with acid to get more phosphorus to release. The acid is not organic and can suppress microorganisms in the soil so that makes it a chemical fertilizer. All fertilizer bags are required to label the percentages of N P K: Nitrogen, Phosphorus and Potassium. They are expressed in percentages of each nutrient that is in that bag. These three nutrients NPK are usually going to be lower in organic fertilizers than chemical fertilizers but the advantage of organic fertilizers is that you are increasing the microbe population in the soil and in the long term building better soil.

Fertilizers that carry the OMRI label are a sure way of knowing that a fertilizer is organic. If it does not have the OMRI label and it comes from a natural or organic source it may be organic but you need to ask more Questions.

List of organic fertilizers: This list is grouped by what mineral is most available in each source. They will have other minerals in each one. You don't have to buy these sources as individual ingredients because there are many brands of fertilizers that combine them for you but it is good to know when you are looking at the ingredients on a bag of fertilizer.

Organic fertilizers that contain Nitrogen

Animal Manure: Chicken, Cow or Rabbit (Don't use dog or cat manure or compost from sewage waste in a vegetable garden.)

Fish meal: Dried Fish parts

Fish Emulsion: Fish that is made into liquid. It is better to buy fish hydrolysate because it has not been heated and contains all the beneficial microbes and enzymes.

Insect Manure: From places that raise fish bait like Crickets and worms

Blood Meal: Dried Blood from animals

Feather Meal: Chicken feathers that are ground and composted

Chilean Nitrate: Mined from natural deposits in Chile. There are also other brands that come from nitrogenous rock.

Bat Guano: Bat manure collected where Bats roost

Alfalfa: Dried Alfalfa plants

Cottonseed Meal: From the seed of the cotton plant

Corn Gluten: From Corn

Organic Fertilizers that contain Phosphorus

Rock Phosphate: Mined from the earth, not treated

Calphos: Mined from the earth in Florida it is a combination of calcium and Phosphorus.

Bone Meal: Ground and steamed animal bone

Organic sources of Potassium

Potassium Sulfate: Mined from the earth in several places around the world.

Green sand: Mined from the earth in New Jersey

Organic sources of Calcium

Garden Lime: Limestone mined from the earth. It could be Dolomitic limestone and contain Calcium and Magnesium. It could be called high cal lime and only have a small amount of magnesium. A soil test would dictate which one would be best. Stay away from hydrated lime or quick lime because it could burn your plants.

Gypsum: Mined from the earth and contains calcium and sulfur.

Brand names of mixed Complete Fertilizers

Espoma®

EB Stone®

Neptune Harvest®

Harmony®

Safer®

Fox Farm®

A Word About Compost

Sometimes it can be confusing about what compost really is. In its simplest definition compost is organic matter that is decaying or rotting into a substance that looks nothing like its original form.

Some examples of organic matter would be plants or any of their parts and animals or any of their manure. Anything that was once alive and is now decomposing is organic matter. Cow, horse, rabbit or any manure from plant eating animals is considered safe to compost for use in the vegetable garden but not manure from any meat eating animals like dogs or cats. It is better not to put any meat scraps into your compost pile.

Compost can contain nutrients and minerals derived from what it was originally. It also may be loaded with billions of microbes that are very beneficial to plants.

Not all compost is the same because of what it was made from and how it was made. The best compost is made from nutrient rich materials and is composted with what is called the hot composting method. To make this kind of compost requires the correct moisture (damp but not soggy), one part green materials called the nitrogen (like green grass or vegetable scraps) and 4 parts brown material called the carbon (like wood or dried leaves). The particles need to be small and air needs to be available to all parts of the compost pile usually accomplished by turning it every few days. The microbe population builds up and so does the heat as you turn the pile sometimes reaching 140 degrees F. As the pile cools down it is turned again so more air gets in and temperatures go up again. This causes the compost pile to breakdown very quickly. The finished compost is complete when the pile stops heating up and what is left resembles black soil. This method takes anywhere from a few weeks to a couple of months. This is the best compost and the hardest to find. That is why many gardeners will make their own compost to be sure where the materials came from and how it was composed.

The cool compost method is what happens when you pile up your organic matter and just wait on it to rot down on its own. This may take one year or many years depending on how big the pieces of organic matter are. For example logs take longer than chopped up leaves. This compost is valuable but not as good as the compost made from a hot pile method.

Takeaway Points

Here are the key points that I want you to remember about soil:

▶ You want your soil to be alive with lots of microorganisms. You get that from compost and worm castings and by never using chemical fertilizers that will kill the microbes.

▶ Keeping your soil at a PH of around 6.5 will increase your microbial life and mineral absorption by the plants

▶ Keep the soil covered with mulch or cover crops to protect it from erosion and feed the microbial life. (Always have something covering the soil)

▶ Don't over till the soil. Some tilling may be necessary but less is better.

▶ It is easier to correct drainage issues before you start your garden

▶ Make your decision early on about whether to use native mineral soil or bagged potting soils

▶ You may need to add an organic fertilizer to get enough nutrients for your plant needs for healthy growth

▶ Most any compost has value for growing plants but compost made from nutrient rich ingredients and composted in a hot pile is the best

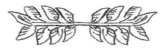

Step 4: What to Plant, When

Genesis 8:22 English Standard Version (ESV)
22 While the earth remains, seed time and harvest, cold and heat,
summer and winter, day and night, shall not cease."

7.25.17. GEN

Everything has a season. This is true in many areas of life and very true with plants. We can try to plant heat loving summer vegetables in the cold winter but it does not work very well. It is so much easier and the plants grow so much better when we just give the plant what it wants. So you have the question "how do I know what the plant wants." Fortunately other gardeners have come before us and we have sources of information that we can look up to find out what temperature and other environmental conditions a plant will grow best in.

Online Resources

Most states have available through their agricultural universities a vegetable gardening planner that will give you a guide to what you can plant when. For where I live in Georgia that is the University of Georgia and their vegetable garden planner can be found on the web at:

> http://extension.uga.edu/publications/files/html/C963/
> C963VegeChart.pdf

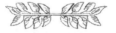

Seed Catalogs

Seed catalogs are also a good source of information and some better than others. I refer to Johnny's Select Seeds catalog. Even though they are based in Maine which is a long way from Georgia their information is still valuable to me.

You want to look at the general cultural information for different types of vegetables. That will tell you what the ideal germination temperature will be as well as what the ideal growing environment is. Each different variety or cultivar within each kind of vegetable will also have days to maturity that is either from the time you plant the seed or from the time the seedling goes into the garden. Be sure to check to see which they are referring to.

This is important because that will tell you if you have enough time to grow and harvest that vegetable before it get too cold or too hot for it to grow.

Climate Conditions

Knowing the climate conditions where you garden is important. Things like the average first frost of the fall and the average last frost in the spring is something every gardener needs to commit to memory for your particular area. Local factors like large bodies of water and elevation can have an influence so ask some local gardeners what their experience has been. You can also find that information from your State Agricultural University.

We have a long growing season on my Farm just south of Atlanta GA. (USDA hardies zone 8) We can grow something year round if we provide a little protection with row covers. Our main growing seasons are spring, summer and fall with spring and fall having mostly the same plants.

The following is what I plant when and will work for most of the southeastern United States.

Early Spring Garden

On my farm in Georgia I plant our early spring garden around March 1st. Frost can still be expected but we have many warm days. I look at the weather reports very closely for nights that dip down to 35 degrees Fahrenheit and below and I am ready to cover plants with a row cover cloth on those nights to protect them from frost. High winds can also be expected during this time so keeping these covers on the plants can be a challenge. I prefer using the spun material sold as row cover as opposed to plastic because it is easier to work with and will not over heat as quickly the next day if the sun comes out bright and sunny. It also is easier to keep in place in high winds.

A rule of thumb that was passed down to me was that if the high temperature for the day is added to the low temperature of the day and that number is above 100 then plants that are grown in cool months of the year will put on growth during those days. The reason you are trying to get your early spring garden planted as soon as possible and going through all the trouble of covering and uncovering is that the plants you are planting in an early spring garden will not tolerate the hot days of summer. They need to be planted and harvested before the temperatures start exceeding 85 degrees Fahrenheit consistently. Planting early maturing varieties is also a way to get in an early spring garden in areas of the country where the spring season is short.

I divide my list of vegetables to grow into three seasons Early Spring, summer and fall. Then I decide what I will direct seed into the garden and those that I will put into the garden as plants. I have always liked starting with plants when I can because I have a head start on the season but some things like carrots just don't transplant well. If you are a new gardener and unsure about whether to start with seeds or plants I would say that plants are easier for most vegetables except root crops. I would also tell you that you should not be afraid to plant seeds because you will not always be able to find the plants you want. Also growing your own transplants indoors or in a greenhouse is fun and opens up a wider variety of neat vegetables that you can grow yourself. Your selection at the local garden shops may be limited to a few standard varieties of vegetables.

You can also direct seed them into the garden as well but because our spring is short in Georgia I like to get started with plants when I can so that they will mature before hot weather arrives in May and June.

I also look for varieties of vegetables that will mature in 60 days or less. In my Gardening area (Zone 8) it gets hot early in the spring months and we need early maturing cool weather crops to beat the arrival of hot weather.

You will find how many days a particular vegetable needs to mature in your seed catalogs. This is called DM or days to maturity.

My list of early spring vegetables that I plant into the garden as plants:

This is my list and you may find other vegetables that grow in the cooler months of the year in your area. Refer to your seed catalog to see if the vegetable you want to grow will tolerate cool temperatures.

Broccoli

Broccoli Raab

Cabbage

Chinese Cabbage

Cauliflower

Kale

Lettuce

Spinach

Bok Choy

Swiss chard

Arugula

Sugar Snap Peas

Collards

Kohlrabi

Fennel

My list of early spring vegetable that I grow from seed:

Mainly because these vegetables are grown for their roots and don't transplant well

Soil temperatures need to be a least 55 degrees F for these direct seeded vegetables to sprout.

Turnips

Beets

Carrots

Radishes

Potatoes (Irish potatoes are grown from eyes of a potato and not actually a seed.)

Summer Vegetables

These plants like the hot summer weather and should be planted after all danger of frost is over. You can cover if you have a late frost but don't try to plant too early because it is not just about the late frost but how warm the soil is. Sometimes if the soil temperatures are in the low 60's your summer vegetables are just not going to grow very well

I plant these plants after the average last frost in the spring which is usually in the first two weeks of April for me. You can check local weather information to find your average last frost date where you garden. For summer vegetables I have found it better to be a week or two later than planned than to plant too early when we are having a cool spring.

My list of summer warm season vegetables that I put into the garden as plants:

Tomatoes

Peppers

Eggplant

Okra and Sweet Potatoes in early May

Plants started indoors and moved to the garden:

The following list can be planted directly into the soil when the soil temperature is above 65 degrees F but sometimes I start them as plants indoors before moving to the garden as it gives me a couple of weeks head start. All these Vegetables transplant well from plants as well as seeding direct into the garden.

Squash

Cilantro

Beans

Okra

Corn

Cucumbers

Melons

Black-eyed peas and other beans (for eating fresh and drying)

I plant some of these vegetables several times during the season like beans, peas, squash and melons so they can harvested over a longer period of time. This is called succession planting.

Fall vegetables

Even though these are fall vegetables you need to plant them in late summer so that you can harvest them in the fall. Late summer for me is late August so they have time to mature before a hard freeze comes. Again I select varieties that mature in around 60 days. The exception to that is Brussels Sprouts which take around 100 days so they need to be planted as plants the first of August in my area.

Vegetables planted in late summer:

The following is a list of vegetables that I put into the garden as plants in late summer to harvest in the fall.

Broccoli	Bok Choy
Broccoli Raab	Swiss Chard
Brussels Sprouts	Sugar Snap Peas
Cabbage	Collards
Chinese Cabbage	Kale
Cauliflower	Asian greens
Kale	Kohlrabi
Lettuce	Fennel
Spinach	

Direct seeding in September:

The following list is plants that I direct seed into the garden in September and harvest later in the fall. I check soil temperatures and try to plant when temperatures are below 85 degrees F. These are root vegetables that don't transplant well or things that are planted close together like baby greens and mature quickly.

Turnips

Beets

Carrots

Mixed baby greens including Kale, Mustard, Bok choy and Lettuce

Radishes

Mustard greens

Turnip greens

Spinach

Arugula

Two other plants:

Two other things that I always plant in the fall (October and November)

Garlic (planted from garlic cloves)
Onions planted from onion plants.

These are not harvested in the fall but in my area they overwinter and are harvested in the spring. Onions can also be planted in the spring.

Takeaway Points

Key points to remember about Step 4.

▶ Check locally if you are unfamiliar with what to plant when. Some good sources would be the local extension service of your state agricultural university, local gardeners, Master gardeners, local garden clubs and local nurseries. Local farmers that you meet at the farmers market are all good sources.

▶ Always be prepared to cover plants in the spring because there might be an unexpected cold snap or late frost.

▶ Use your seed catalog to find out how many days to maturity it takes to grow a crop either from seed or from plants. Based on your climate decide when the best time to harvest a particular crop is and count backwards to find your planting date.

▶ Not every vegetable will do well in your climate. There is nothing wrong with trying new or hard to grow varieties but limit those things to a small amount of your gardening space and grow more of the vegetables you like to eat and that do well in your area.

▶ If there is a particular vegetable that you enjoy and want more of think about having multiple planting dates so that you can harvest over a longer period of time and not all at once. This is called succession planting.

Step 5: Weeds, Water, and Mulch

Genesis 3:17 New International Version (NIV)
To Adam he said, "Because you listened to your
wife and ate fruit from the tree about which
I commanded you,
'You must not eat from it,'
"Cursed is the ground because of you;
through painful toil you will eat food from it
all the days of your life."

Now I really don't feel like as a farmer my ground is cursed but I do know as long as we try to grow something to eat there will be struggles to grow it. Just as in the rest of life it is not always easy.

When you grow up on a farm you talk about the crops and the animals and the weeds and how much it is raining or not raining. You are close to it and your livelihood depends on these things. Some of the things I remember people saying when I was growing up were things like:

"The only way we will ever get rid of nut grass is if we move off and leave it."

"It is so dry that we will have to feed the cows pine straw to keep their guts from sticking together"

"If it was not for weeds that farmer could not get anything to grow in his garden"

"I am praying for the July rains to save my corn crop but don't let it rain when I am baling hay."

"I could not have sown those weeds that thick even if I had tried"

"It is so hot and dry the grass is crunching under our feet"

"It's so wet the ducks are looking for higher ground"

So even if the weather and the weeds don't cooperate don't give up on your garden. Have the attitude of the farmer that next year is always going to be better.

You may ask why there are three things in step 5. It is because if you mulch your garden bed you will have to water and weed less.

Think about mulch as the blanket you spread over your garden bed just like you have a cover over yourself in your bed. It is not the organic matter that you mix into the soil but rather the layer that covers the soil.

You can use many materials as mulch for your garden but I like to use mulches that are chopped up and will mostly rot back into the soil over a season. The smaller the mulching material is the easier it is to tuck it around plants so I like to use chopped leaves or small bark or wood chips.

Benefits from Mulching

▶ Mulch keeps the plant roots cooler in summer and warmer in winter.

▶ Mulch will slow down evaporation so you don't have to water as much.

▶ Mulch will keep weed seeds from sprouting.

▶ Mulch will cut down on soil borne diseases by keeping soil from splashing up on the leaves.

▶ Mulch adds organic matter and nutrients back to the soil as it decomposes.

▶ Mulch encourages earthworms to live in your garden which is a good thing.

▶ Mulches like cedar and eucalyptus chips can repel certain insects.

▶ Mulch makes any weeds that do make their way into your garden easier to pull up.

When to Mulch

Timing is important when mulching. You want to have a weed free bed when you apply your mulch because mulch will smother seeds better than weeds that are already sprouted. You can mulch your garden bed before you plant. You may need to till the soil initially and prepare your soil with any amendments like fertilizer or lime before you add mulch. Add at least 3 to 4 inches of mulch over your prepared soil. If you keep your plants mulched then the soil will stay soft under the mulch. The soil under the mulch can be so soft that you don't have to re-till the soil to plant the next crop. A no till or low till garden has many benefits and mulching will be a key component in this method. If you ever find that you do have to re-till your soil you will want to rake any mulch that has not rotted off to the side and put it back on top after the soil is prepared. If you are applying anything like lime or organic fertilizer and not tiling your soil again you can simply apply those things to the top of the mulch.

When you are planting seed into the garden pull back the mulch to expose enough bare soil to get your seeds into the soil. After the seed has sprouted begin to move the mulch back around your seedling a little at time being careful not to bury them completely. When you are putting plants into your garden bed you can move a little of the mulch to the side and after you plant into the soil below then tuck the mulch back around the plant.

I know some gardeners like to till the soil and cultivate the soil around the plants to keep the garden weed free and that method will work. The mulching method is presented here as an alternative that I have seen work and save time and effort.

Weeds

Mulching will eliminate most of the weeds in your garden beds but you will have weeds sometimes despite your best efforts. The best way to deal with weeds is to be consistent about removing them when they are small.

A small weed is easier to pull and when you pull it out soon enough it has not had a chance to produce any additional seed. Weeds that are growing in heavy mulch are also easier to pull than weeds in garden soil.

Starting off weed free is the first step to keeping weeds out of your garden bed. Look out for perennial weeds when you are first preparing your beds. Hard to kill grasses like Bermuda grass and perennial weeds (those weeds that come back from year to year from underground roots) should get the most attention when you are first preparing your garden beds. Dig these hard to control weeds out by the root early on and it will save you so much work later on.

After starting off weed free the next thing to pay attention to is not to bring weed seeds into the garden bed. Sometimes things like hay and grass clippings can seem like a good idea only to find out they were loaded with weed seeds. If you are not sure if the mulch you are adding to the garden is weed free or not put it in a pile and keep it moist until you are satisfied that no weeds are coming up in your mulch. Some mulching materials that are relatively weed free include leaves, pine straw, wood chips and bark chips.

Keeping the surrounding areas mowed is another way to keep weed seeds from spreading to your garden beds. Also make sure that when you mow around your garden you are discharging the grass from the lawn mower away from your garden beds.

Water

There will always be times when you need to water your plants but mulch will definitely cut back on the need to water your garden as often. Mulch helps to slow evaporation and keeps the soil at an even temperature. The times when plants need to be watered the most is when they are first planted and during periods of drought. An established plant will go for a week or more without being watered if it is mulched well. The exception to this is when you have plants in containers because the soil volume is smaller than the volume of soil in garden beds.

To know when you need to water plants the best way is to feel of the soil by sticking your finger into the soil to the second knuckle. You can also take a pinch of soil and squeeze it between your finger and thumb. If you can squeeze a drop of water from the soil you don't need to water.

Check your plants water needs often because plants that stress because of lack of water will not provide you with the harvest you want. Plants that are under stress are also more susceptible to insects and diseases.

When it is necessary to apply water to your garden bed you

want to apply water directly to the soil and the roots and don't wet the leaves of the plant. Wet leaves will lead to disease.

The best way to apply the water to the garden beds is either by hand watering with a nozzle pointed directly at the soil underneath the leaves or with a drip or soaker hose. It is always better to soak your garden bed thoroughly than to just wet the top inch or two of soil. Small garden beds can be watered by hand with a watering can but you will have to decide if you have enough time for this method.

I encourage gardeners to use either soaker hoses or a drip irrigation system on their garden beds. Either of these can connect directly to a garden hose and an inexpensive timer can be added as well. The easer you make it to water the more likely you will do it in a timely manner. A timer will help greatly especially if you are short on time or you are going to be away from your garden for a few days. The investment you make upfront for a watering system will pay for itself in the long run.

Takeaway Points

Key points to take away from Step 5

▶ Mulch will cut back on the amount of time spent weeding and watering your garden

▶ Use mulches that have smaller pieces that will tuck in around plants and decompose faster.

▶ Start with a weed free garden bed and pull out new weeds when they are small.

▶ Keep areas surrounding the garden mowed to discourage new weed seeds from coming into the garden bed.

▶ Don't wet the leaves of the plant when watering.

▶ A drip watering system with a timer will pay for itself in the long run.

Step 6: Pest and Diseases

Psalm 50:11 New International Version (NIV)
I know every bird in the mountains,
and the insects in the fields are mine.

Being an organic Farmer I have learned to come to terms with insects. I don't always like them and sometimes they can make me mad. I have always said if you are growing something good to eat or pretty to look at there is a critter out there that wants to eat it too. When you are trying to grow things in a natural way you must look at what is happening out in the natural world and then try to mimic it instead of always trying to hit it over the head with a bigger hammer.

I have been brought all kinds of bugs to identify for people. They would come to me with their little baggies of bugs and sometimes they did not even have them in a bag. I guess they wanted to share their misery with me by spreading the bugs to my plants. I would always try to identify them the best I could and it made me a little more knowledgeable in my bug ID.

The thing to remember when you are having a bug problem is that something is out of balance. Maybe you have sprayed to kill the bad bugs and killed all the good bugs that would have kept the bad bugs from getting out of control. Or you have over-fertilized your plants and made them susceptible to a bug invasion. Sometimes it is just the overall environment that may be beyond our control like weather or it may be that since we have been kicked out of the Garden of Eden we are going to have struggles with growing our plants.

At any rate bugs on our plants are a fact of life and we have to learn to be smart enough to deal with them.

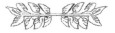

Three levels of defense to control harmful insects and diseases in the garden:

I look at controlling insects and diseases at three different levels. Each one more aggressive as you go from one to three. I think this is a good way to look at it because even organic dusts and sprays can have negative effects on beneficial insects and the environment. We should not just substitute an organic spray for a chemical one but rather take a holistic approach to gardening where you do everything you can to make the plant as healthy as you can.

First Line of Defense

First line of defense is growing a healthy plant.

A healthy plant growing in good soil with adequate sunlight and water that has been planted at the correct time of the year will fight off many insects and diseases on its own.

Selecting plants that grow well in your climate will go a long way toward avoiding problems with insects and diseases. In the southeast where my farm is located we have an extended period of heat and high humidity that limits some of our choices when selecting vegetables to grow. We can only grow plants that like the cool weather either in the fall or spring.

I will choose these cool weather varieties that have 60 days or less to maturity so that I can fit them in during our short, mild growing conditions. Trying to grow these cool weather varieties like broccoli or sugar snap peas in the heat of the summer will only invite problems.

In northern parts of the country where the summers are short you might have problems growing heat loving plants like black eyed peas or okra. Just like trying to fit a square peg in a round hole some plants are not going to do well in a climate they don't like. If you are having trouble growing a particular vegetable in your climate maybe just take the hint and grow something that performs well where you garden.

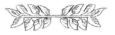

Cultural Requirements

Make sure that you refer to the plants cultural requirements when selecting plants to grow in your garden beds.

In the hot humid south diseases can be very difficult to overcome. The best action is to prevent disease before it starts. Plants that are in full sun with lots of air circulation will be less prone to diseases. Air circulation will help to keep the leaves drier and cut down on the spread of diseases .Many diseases cannot spread when the leaves are dry. Of course proper fertilization is important because too much nitrogen will cause excessive growth and lead to more disease. Mulching around the base of the plant with dried leaves or wood chips will keep water from splashing soil particles on the leaves that can carry disease. Always water plants at the base of the plant and as much as possible avoid getting the leaves wet. Pruning out some of the side shoots or suckers will cut down on the thick growth that keeps interior leaves from staying wet longer. This will increase air circulation around leaves to dry them quickly after a rain or heavy dew.

If we grow something that is pretty to look at or good to eat there is a critter around that wants to eat it too. Sometimes that may be a larger critter like a deer or a rabbit but what I am talking about here are the small critters that are harder to see and identify. It is important if you're going to be a gardener that you learn to identify at least the more common insects.

Most insects are not harmful to your plants and only a few

are doing any damage but those few will do a lot of damage if left unchecked. Looking at the damage that they leave on the plant will give you a clue as to what kind of insect you have. If there are holes in the leaf or parts of the leaf are missing then you have bugs with chewing mouth parts and they are usually somewhat larger. If the plant has lost its good color and looks pale or has puckered leaves then you may have an insect that is sucking the juice from the plant. These insects are much smaller and harder to see because they hide under the leaves. We may not see them until a lot of damage is done.

Either way you need to be scouting for insects several times a week to find them in the early stages. Looking on the undersides of the leaf and around the base of the plant is important. If it is a hot day some of the chewing insects will hide during the heat of the day so checking early in the morning or late in the evening will be a better strategy.

Internet Help for Identifying Insects

There are many sites on the internet that can help you learn to identify insects. Arbico-organics.com is a good place to start.

Hand Picking

Hand picking is a first line of insect control that some gardeners use. At the first sight of insects you can pick off beetles and caterpillars and other bugs that are easy to see and handle. This works if you have a small garden or they are not too many bugs. Have a small pail of soapy water and as you pick off the insects drop them into the pail.

Sometimes in the beginning of the season when there are not too many we hand pick squash bug eggs because they are in small round red clusters and easy to see. A direct blast of water from the garden hose is also sometimes effective.

Exclusion

Exclusion is another first line of defense. Use row covers over your vegetable beds to exclude the insects. Row cover is also called a floating row cover. It is a light weight spun material that light can penetrate. On crops that don't need to be pollinated covering the entire plant with row cover will keep insects out. This works well for leafy green crops like lettuce and kale, any plants that don't require pollination to set a fruit before harvesting. Plants like cucumber and squash can be covered in the early stages of growth but the cover has to be removed as soon as they start blooming in order for insect pollinators to reach them to be pollinated and set fruit.

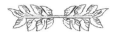

Row Covers

Row covers work best if they have some type of frame over the garden bed for the cover to rest on. Caution should be taken in extreme hot weather because it can heat up too much under the cover for some crops.

Traps and Lures

Insect traps and lures are a good way to trap and monitor insect problems. Many traps use pheromones, lures and baits that contain sticky substances on different colored surfaces that will attract specific types of insects. Trapping your pests not only decreases the population but also makes you more aware of their presence. Arbico-organics .com is a good source for many of these traps and lures.

Second Line of Defense

The Second line of defense is to invite good bugs into your garden.

As an organic gardener you want to invite the good bugs into your garden that will eat some if not all of the bad bugs. You can do this by planting more herbs and flowers. Be sure to plant flowers and herbs that have lots of nectar that good bugs are drawn to. We plant Bronze Fennel, Dill, Parsley, Zinnias, and Sunflowers. We even let some of our leafy green vegetable crops go to flower like lettuce and collards. Any plant that is labeled as a butterfly attractor will usually attract beneficial insects. You may not think of paper wasp as being good for your garden but they will eat a lot of caterpillars that eat holes in your plants so if they are not directly in my way where I think someone may get stung I always leave them alone. There are other small parasitic wasp and flies that are very small and don't sting people. This wasp will hunt down destroy many plant eating bugs. Learn what these wasp look like and plant flowers and herbs that will attract them to your garden.

You can also buy and release beneficial insects like green lacewings, lady bugs and parasitic wasps into your garden but you have to have the right habitat for them before releasing them or they won't stay. This means that you need to plant some of the following food sources for your beneficial insects.

Using herbs and Flowers

Some herbs and flowers we plant on our Farm to Attract Beneficial Insects and Bees.

Basil	Bronze Fennel
Buckwheat	Sweet Fennel
Clover	Jerusalem Artichoke
Comfrey	Mexican Sunflower
Coreopsis	Milk weed
Cosmos	Vetch
Dill	Yarrow
Elderberry	Zinnias

Mother Earth News has a good resource on what to plant to attract the good bugs.

http://www.motherearthnews.com/organic-gardening/ pest-control/plants-to-attract-beneficial-insects-zl0z1005zvau

Third Line of Defense

The third line of defense is using organic dust and sprays.

Despite our best efforts we can still have an outbreak of harmful insects and instead of turning to synthetic chemicals you can use organic remedies.

The most gentle of these remedies is to use soaps or sprays made from plants like the neem tree seed to make oil. Soaps made from plant and animal fats can be very effective in killing insects as long as they don't contain detergents.

There are also dusts like Diatomaceous Earth that cut and dry out the insect's body. These are safe to use and easy on the beneficial insects.

You can also use biological controls that are derived from naturally occurring microbes. Biological Sprays that contain bacteria like Spinosad and BT that target certain types of insects. You need to be more careful with these and not spray when your bees and other pollinators are out.

As a last resort when I have very difficult to control insects I use Organic Pyrethrum that comes from the chrysanthemum flower. This is very toxic to all insects and should be used carefully. Spray late in the evening around sundown to avoid harming bees.

So to recap when it is necessary to use organic sprays and dust I use the least harmful to the environment first. If I can't get control then I move on to the more aggressive remedies.

With any of these remedies you need to cover the entire plant, even under the leaves where insects can hide. It is best to use a pump up sprayer that makes enough pressure to create a fine mist. You can add a teaspoon of insecticidal soap to other organic sprays to make them more effective.

Organic Insect control from least toxic
to beneficial insects to most toxic

Lures and traps to monitor the insect population

Sprays of pepper or garlic that repel

Insecticidal soap (use pure soap without detergents)

Neem Oil

DE or Diatomaceous Earth (Dust)

BT or bacillus thuringiensis (very effective on caterpillars)

Spinosad (wide spectrum biological insect control)

Organic Pyrethrum (spray late in the evening to avoid harm to bees)

All Organic sprays and dust should carry the OMRI (Organic Materials Review Institute) label identifying them as an organic product.

These are the organic dust and sprays used to control certain garden insects and diseases but should only be used after the first two levels of defense have not been effective. Any organic spray or dust still has the potential to harm you and beneficial insects so read labels carefully and follow directions.

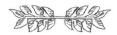

A few common Insects

Aphids: small soft bodied insect sometimes called plant lice. Found mostly on the undersides of the leaf but on the stems as well. Aphids suck the juices from the plant and if their population gets large enough they will distort the shape and color of the leaf. Scout for this small insect by looking on the back side of the leaf. Ants will carry aphids from plant to plant so ants may be an indication of aphids.

Lady bugs and green lace wings: A natural predator so if you have these beneficial insects present wait to see if they can knock the population down. Aphids have a tremendous ability to reproduce quickly so keep a close watch on susceptible plants. Insecticidal soap is a good control but it may take more than one spraying being sure to cover the undersides of the leaves.

Beetles: There are several different types of beetles that damage vegetables. They all have chewing mouth parts and leave holes in the leaf. Some are large like the Japanese beetle and some are small like the flea beetle but they all have a hard outer body shell at the adult stage. They look very different at the immature nymph stage and have soft bodies which are more susceptible to organic controls and predators.

Mexican bean beetle: Nymph stage - Control with Spinosad. Adult stages - Control with a combination of Pyrethrum and Soap.

Colorado potato beetle: Nymph stage - Control with Spinosad. Adult stages – Control with a combination of Pyrethrum and Soap.

Flea beetle: Pyrethrum and soap combination. Also Diatomaceous Earth dust.

Caterpillars: Insects go through different life stages and only harm our plants at certain stages. The butterfly or moth is the adult of many different kinds of caterpillars that eat our plants. The adults will lay eggs on specific types of plants so learn to identify the adult and you will know that after the eggs are laid you should be on the lookout for the caterpillar that is going to do the damage.

Predatory Insects: Beneficial predatory insects like wasp can keep your caterpillars in check. There are times especially in the fall when it is necessary to use organic sprays or dust to control large outbreaks. BT (Bacillus thuringiensis) is very effective in controlling most caterpillars. Spinosad is another good control. Both BT and

Spinosad are types of bacteria making them organic biological insecticides.

White flies: These are tiny white flying insects that suck the juices out of the plant. When their population is small organic remedies like insecticidal soap and neem oil will work but if left unchecked for too long Pyrethrum and soap is a more aggressive approach.

Organic sprays to control diseases

Most common diseases of vegetables are fungus, bacteria, virus and mildew. There is not much that we can do about a virus except for controlling the insects that carry them into the plant. i.e. the cucumber beetle that infects cucumber with cucumber mosaic virus. Organic remedies for bacteria, fungus and mildew include:

Organic sprays to control diseases:

Pure Soap

Neem Oil

Milk

The next three are the ones I use the most for diseases

Potassium Bicarbonate

Serenade (biological control of diseases)

Organic copper

Takeaway Points

Key points to take away in step 6.

▶ Research the plants you are growing before you plant so that you know what insects are likely to attack them.

▶ Make a plan to deal with bugs before they take over. Introduce beneficial insects or have the appropriate organic dust or spray on hand in case you need it.

▶ Keep your plants healthy. Grow your plants with the correct light, water and nutrients.   Also always plant the right plant in the correct season.

▶ Scout for insects regularly.

▶ Yellow sticky traps and pheromone traps will capture insects to let you know which ones are present so that you can take appropriate action.

▶ Know which insects and diseases to be on the lookout for.

▶ Learn to identify insects and diseases correctly.

▶ Plant flowers and herbs to encourage beneficial insects.

▶ Use exclusion using light weight row cover.

▶ Hand pick into a pail of soapy water.

▶ Use a strong stream of water from the hose. This is the least toxic remedy to control insects and diseases.

▶ Prune off leaves with black spots when they first appear.

▶ Increase air circulation by using correct spacing when planting disease prone plants.

▶ Be willing to accept some damage to plants to allow your beneficial insects to have a chance to control the problem before moving on to organic sprays or dusts.

▶ You have to determine the threshold of damage that you are willing to accept.

Step 7: Harvest

Mark 4:29 (NIV)
"As soon as the grain is ripe, he puts the sickle to it, because the harvest has come."

The big question is when do I pick it? And as I have heard others say when it is ready it is ready. But how do you know when it's ready? It may be ready when you are out of town or it may be ready when you're busy. It is not ready when you wait with anticipation for it to get ripe it, is ready when it is ready.

When I was growing up we would have vegetables to cook and can in the summer but it always seemed that there would always be too much ready at one time. My dad would plant a big garden with the tractor in the spring. All the time my mother would be saying this is too much garden. She knew that it would be up to her to pick and preserve the abundant harvest later that summer and my dad would be on to other things on the farm. At one time there were canneries run by local or state governments where you could go and can things on an industrial scale into tin cans. Each family would bring their vegetables and prepare them in these big kitchens and once they put them into the cans the workers at the cannery would take over and put on the lids and put them through the big industrial canners and you could pick them up once they cooled. I am not sure if any of these canneries still exist. I know the ones we used to go to have been closed long ago.

My advice to you is to plan your planting according to your vegetable needs. If you don't want to preserve your vegetables plant according to your weekly vegetable needs plus maybe some to share. If you want to preserve some food for later plant enough plants to furnish vegetables to give you plenty for that. We never know from one year to the next exactly what the garden will produce because weather, insects and disease affect it too much, but plan like you are not going to have those problems.

We furnish vegetables for customers to buy at the farm year round but the bulk of the production is 36 weeks. To do this we do what is called succession planting. This means that certain things are planted multiple times over several weeks. This works well for crops that produce everything at one time like bush type green beans, tomatoes, melons, corn, lettuce, carrots, beets and annual herbs like cilantro and dill.

The seasons of the year will also spread out the harvest because the spring and the fall can be used to grow crops that do well in cool weather and the summer for warm season crops. In most parts of the country it is possible to grow various types of vegetables 12 months of the year with some protection.

Knowing when a vegetable is ripe can take some practice.

Harvesting your own vegetables is the goal of every vegetable gardener but if not done correctly or at the right time it can result in poor quality vegetables.

Tips for Harvesting

Here are some tips you can use when you go to harvest your crops.

▶ Harvest often and don't let vegetables get too large.

▶ If you harvest when leaves are wet you may be spreading diseases from one plant to the next. But harvesting during the cool morning hours is good but the wet dew may still on the plant. What is a gardener to do? (The best you can.)

▶ Use a knife or a pair of scissors to cut vegetables from the plants so as not to tear the stems.

▶ Don't leave vegetables out in the sun after harvesting them. Try to keep them in the shade as you pick.

▶ Cool vegetables down quickly in cool water or in the refrigerator as soon after harvest as possible.

▶ Read up on the varieties of vegetables that you are growing so that you will know the best size to harvest at.

Asparagus: Harvest young shoots 6 to 8 inches long as they appear in the spring. The season is short so enjoy them while you can. Be patient because you will not harvest the first crop until the second or third spring but because it is a long lived plant it will provide spring shoots for many years.

Beans, Snap: We are talking about green beans here. The green bean needs to full but tender with the bean inside not fully developed. They should snap into easily and some varieties will have a fiber string attached that can be removed when you snap off the ends.

If you have a few that have developed a bean inside (my Mom calls these shuckey) shell out the bean and add it to the pot and add the outer shell to your compost.

Beans, Lima: Or if you grew up where I did we called them Butter Beans. Butter beans are ready to harvest when the pods are bulging with thick mature beans inside or as my momma would say don't pick um unless they are filled out.

Try shelling a few and you will understand. Left too long on the plant and they will start to turn yellow and dry out.

Beets: They can be harvested as baby beets the size of a quarter up to a half dollar or as full grown beets around 2 to 3 inches in diameter. You may want to thin your crop of beets by taking out every other one as baby beets and then let the rest mature into full size. The leaves of the beet are best used fresh.

They can be cooked or used raw in salads. I had to learn to like the earthy taste because Judy said they were good for me.

Bok Choy: This crunchy form of Chinese cabbage grows fast and can be harvested at almost any size from a baby green 2 inches across to a full head 8 to 10 inches tall. Read about the many varieties in your seed catalog and how you are going to use it to know at what size you should harvest.

Broccoli: You should cut your broccoli heads when they are still compact before any flower buds open. What you are eating is the flower bud and about 6" of the stem under it. Depending on the variety and how well your broccoli grew the head, it will be 6 to 8 inches across.

After harvesting the center head you will have smaller side shoots that you can harvest but they will get smaller over a few weeks. Not many people harvest the leaves but they are very good and can be prepared like you would collards.

A lot of people don't cook the stem of the broccoli but are missing out on lots of flavor. You peel it and chop for steaming or eating raw.

Brussels sprouts: These tiny cabbage looking sprouts grow along the stem usually about 1 to 2 inches across they are best harvested in the cold part of the year to give them the best flavor.

You can start harvesting individual sprouts from the ground up or cut the top out of the plants when they have reached a mature height and they will tend to mature more uniformly.

The leaves are tasty as well. Many of our customers say that they are their favorite winter greens.

Cabbage: Cut just below the heads when they are firm and the appropriate size for the variety that you are growing. Best to grow them so they can be harvested in the cooler parts of the year.

Carrot: You can dig carrots when they are small for baby carrots 1/4 to 1/2 inches. Try thinning your carrots on the first harvest by taking out every other one. This will leave room for the ones remaining to mature to an inch or so diameter.

In warmer weather carrots will keep growing so don't let them get too big or they will lose their sweet tender taste. Carrots that mature in the winter months will last in the ground much longer and as long as the ground is mulched or covered during hard freezes this is a good way to store them.

Cantaloupe: (Muskmelons) When you gently pull the melon from the vine a ripe cantaloupe is said to slip or come off the vine easily.

The other sign that it is ripe is the netting or outer skin will turn beige and the end that is not attached to the vine (the blossom end) will be soft and have a sweet smell.

Honey dew melons will become pale in color but don't always slip as easily.

Cauliflower: This cool weather crop produces just one head per plant and no side shoots like broccoli.

Harvest your heads of cauliflower when they are firm and white about 6 to 8 inches across. Don't wait too long to harvest or they will become loose and begin to look like little piles of rice that are poor eating quality.

You need to eat it or freeze it right away because it will not last long in the refrigerator.

Chard: Cut the entire leaf including the stem when they are less than 12 inches long.

Individual outside leaves can be cut from this plant over a long period of time making it very productive.

Take care to move chard leaves into refrigeration quickly as they will wilt in the heat. You can submerse the freshly cut end of the leaves into a shallow container of water like you would a cut flower when you put them in the refrigerator to help keep them fresh.

Collard: I know that Kale gets all the attention but collard is kale's first cousin. You can cut the entire plant once it is mature but I get more production by harvesting the individual outside leaves as soon as they are about as big as your hand. My Mom always said the best tasting collards came after they had a good frost on them. Growing up in the south I have eaten more than my share of this tasty green. Kale has its place but don't ignore the collard.

Corn: Sweet corn is harvested when the ears are filled out and the kernels are still milky when you puncture them with your thumb nail. This happens about 20 days after the silks appear on the ear. The silks will turn slightly brown and you can check a few ears for tenderness and fullness.

Wait too long and your corn will lose it sweetness. Plan to eat or freeze it within a couple of days of harvest and cool it off as quickly as you can after picking.

Resist the temptation to open every ear because it last longer if you keep it cold and tight in the shuck.

Cucumber: Check your seed catalog for the best size to harvest at because there are different sizes, colors and shapes of cucumbers. Harvesting at the younger appropriate size will give the best texture and taste.

Don't just plant one variety and experiment with the ones you don't always find in the supermarket.

Eggplant: Pick when they are full size according to the variety that you are growing. They should be full size and have a glossy skin.

Cut the stem with a sharp knife or shears so as not to damage the plant.

Garlic: Harvest the bulb when most of the leaves have turned brown. In Georgia that is sometime in early summer.

Dig the bulbs in the morning when rain is not likely and let the sun dry them during the day.

Move the garlic to a covered area and lay them out on screens to continue drying. When the bulbs are completely dry in 2 to 3 weeks brush off the dirt but don't wash them.

Use any damaged bubs right away the rest will store in a dry covered area for several months.

Fennel: Sweet fennel will have a white base with long wispy tops. You can use the white fleshy part as well as the wispy leaves.

Once the fennel is 2 to 4 inches across you can harvest the whole plant by cutting it off at ground level.

Kale: Kale has definitely had all the good press lately and with good cause. It can be used in a variety of stages of growth. It makes a great addition to a salad as a baby green when harvested at a small 3 inch leaf. We plant Red Russian for baby leaf kale.

You can cut it with a pair of scissors and it will come back several times except in extreme heat of the summer. Or we let kale grow to maturity and harvest the outside leaves when they are 10 to 12 inches long. It is just as delicious at this stage.

There are many varieties of kale to choose from so get out your seed catalog and start reading about what's available.

Kohlrabi: This is a very strange looking plant to some people and if you are old enough to remember what the first Russian Satellite Sputnik looked like you can see a resemblance. Besides being strange looking it tastes great and is one of my favorite vegetables.

The stem of the plant just above the soil will swell to about the size of a tennis ball when it is ready to harvest.

The leaves can also be eaten in a stir fry. Peel the outer skin off the round tennis ball shaped base and eat it raw, stir fry it or roast it.

Lettuce: You can grow different types of lettuce and they are harvested differently.

Head lettuce as the name implies produces a head. Some heads are loose like Bibb and some heads are tight and you also have the upright romaine types. All the head lettuce types are harvested all at once and usually don't regrow.

Loose leaf lettuce can be cut with a sharp knife or scissors and the lettuce will regrow for a time or two. Read your seed catalogs for information on how to best harvest the lettuce you choose.

Okra: Some like it hot and okra is one of them. It will produce its best in the hottest part of the summer.

With okra bigger is NOT better so it has to be picked often, like every other day. You want to pick your pods when they are about the size of your thumb but a little bigger is OK with some varieties as long as the pod is soft and flexible. Any older pods that are left on the plant too long need to be removed so you don't slow down your production.

Discard the big pods unless you like to make little craft projects from the over grown pods. (Just Google it.)

The warning I will give you is to wear a long sleeve shirt and gloves because okra makes most people's skin itch and sting.

Onion, Dry Bulb: The green tops of your onion will start to die when your onions are ready to harvest.

After about 3/4 of the top is brown and fallen over cut off the leaves about 1 to 1-1/2 inches above the bulb. Doing this during a dry time without rain is best.

You can store onions in a mesh bag so they have good air circulation around them. I have even seen people store their onions in pantyhose tying a knot between each onion and hanging them up in cool place. The ideal conditions to store onions are 45 to 55 degrees and 50 to 60 percent humidity. Don't worry if you don't have the ideal conditions because not many gardeners do. The best cool well ventilated place you have will work and keep in mind that sweet onions don't store as long as hotter onions.

Onion Green: Just as the name implies these are young green onions that have not formed a bulb.

Sometimes these onions are referred to as pencil onions because of their shape.

Harvest these onions when the tops are 6 to 8 inches tall. They can be stored in the crisper of the refrigerator in plastic bags for up to 2 weeks.

Peas, English: Gardening in the south I never knew much about English peas except they come from a can and did not taste very good. But once I started growing them in my own garden I fell in love with their flavor.

In Georgia we only have a short window of opportunity in the spring and fall to grow them but they are well worth it. Read about the different varieties in your seed catalog because some are grown to be shelled when the pea inside is full and before it starts to turn yellow. Others like sugar snap peas are grown for their edible pods when they are about 3 inches long. And snow peas are still flat when they are ready to harvest.

Peas, Southern: (Black-eyed, Crowder, Zipper, Purple Hull) These are peas that grow in hot humid summers of the southern garden and are one of my favorite vegetables.

They should be harvested when they are swollen in the pod but before the pod begins to turn a lighter cooler and dry out, unless you are going to dry your peas for long term storage.

Fresh peas need to be cooled quickly to remove the field heat and shelled soon after. Keep shelled and unshelled fresh peas in the refrigerator for only a few days before using.

Dried peas can be kept in cool dry place all winter and soaked in water to rehydrate them before cooking.

Peppers: Hot or sweet peppers can be picked green or allowed to turn to their mature color. For the best flavor pick after they have turned colors.

There is a fine line after the peppers change colors before they go bad. Fully ripe peppers will be more susceptible to bacterial and fungus spots. Disease is usually worst in rainy and humid weather.

My strategy is to pick green or slightly turning peppers during times of high disease pressure and allow them to fully ripen during times of lower humidity and lower diseases pressure.

Potato, Irish: Harvest potatoes when they begin to bloom or the tops turn brown and die.

Once you dig your potatoes allow them to dry for a few hours and then store them in a cool dry place out of the sun. Brush off any excess dirt but don't wash them until you are ready to use them.

Potato Sweet: Most sweet potatoes will mature in 90 to 120 days of setting out your plants.

You will need to harvest them before the frost in the fall or it will reduce the quality. Your tubers or potatoes will be 2 to 3 inches in diameter when they are mature depending on variety and how much water was available in the last 30 days of growth.

It is best to cut the vines away just before harvesting. Sweet potatoes need to be cured after digging at temperatures of 85 to 90 degrees F and high humidity. The closest you can keep them to this hot humid environment for two weeks the better any damaged potatoes will heal over and they will also become sweeter.

After two week you can drop the temperature and keep them for several months at cooler temperatures but above 55 degrees F. Don't put them in the refrigerator. Just like Irish potatoes don't wash them until you are ready to use them.

Radish: These are ready to harvest quickly, usually around 4 weeks from the time you put a seed in the ground.

Round varieties should be harvested when they are about an inch in diameter. The bigger radishes will be pithy and have a stronger flavor.

This is a good vegetable to plant in small batches multiple times during the season so you have more of continuous supply. One of our favorite radishes is the variety French Breakfast.

Spinach: You can harvest leaves from 3 to 6 inches long individually by selecting the outer leaves. You can also cut most of the plant above the crown an inch or two above the soil and it will grow back if the weather is not too hot or too cold.

Smaller leaves are more tender for fresh raw salads.

Squash summer: There are many different varieties and shapes of summer squash. The rule of thumb is smaller is usually better.

A guideline for harvesting summer squash would be 6 to 8 inches for zucchini and yellow squash and 2 to 4 inches for round or scallop types. Summer squash will also have a shiny skin when ready.

I like to use a knife to cut the stem so as not to break the vine when harvesting.

Squash winter: Harvest winter squash like butternut when the skin is hard and cannot be punctured with your thumb nail. The skin will appear dull and dry when they are mature.

Store winter squash at around 55 degrees and they will last a couple of months or more.

Tomato: You can leave your tomatoes on the vine until they are fully ripe but still firm before you harvest them. If you are having any diseases or pest issues then they are very susceptible at the fully ripe stage to being damaged so I will sometimes pick when they have turned 75% their mature color and they ripen just fine at around 70 degrees indoors.

I never refrigerate tomatoes because this can reduce the flavor and give them a mealy texture.

Turnip: Harvest purple top turnips when they reach the size of a tennis ball or a little larger.

Salad turnips like the Hakurei variety can be harvested at about an inch or a little larger. They will go bad if left in the ground too long. They also should not be left in the ground during very hot or freezing weather.

Store your turnips in a plastic bag in the refrigerator.

Watermelon: Next to the stem that connects the melon to the vine there is a little curlycue called a tendril and that tendril should be completely brown when the water melon is ripe. The underside of the water melon will turn from white to yellow when it is ready to harvest.

Watermelon will store at room temperature for about a week or in the refrigerator for about 2 to 3 weeks.

Afterword

I hope after reading this book that you have found some things that will help you to be a better gardener. If you garden your entire life you will never know it all and you will be continuously learning because environments change and new varieties become available and no two seasons are ever just alike. So a gardener has to adapt. You will never learn everything from a book so you have to keep gardening to be a good gardener. I really think it is the person that never gives up and has the farmer mentality that next year will be better that makes for a green thumb gardener.

Learn the basics, try new things and pay attention to what is going on in the garden because the plants will let you know how good of a job you are doing! And most of all Enjoy!

Contact Information

Website for the farm and to join our weekly email list:
www.countrygardensfarm.com

Website for organic gardening tips and recipes: www.theteachingfarmers.com

Like us on Facebook at Country Gardens Farm.

Mike and Judy are available to speak to your group on the topics of Growing, Cooking and Preserving Good Food.

Contact us at mikec@countrygardensfarm.com